Original title:
Dreaming in the Dell

Copyright © 2025 Creative Arts Management OÜ
All rights reserved.

Author: Mariana Leclair
ISBN HARDBACK: 978-1-80567-292-0
ISBN PAPERBACK: 978-1-80567-591-4

Flickers of Joy Beneath the Old Oak

In a shady nook, squirrels did play,
Chasing their tails in a charming ballet.
A rabbit in glasses, quite out of sorts,
Read funny novels for all his reports.

The breeze whispered secrets, oh so absurd,
While frogs in the pond croaked out a third.
They crooned about crickets who danced in the grass,
And boasted of giggles that always would last.

A hedgehog in bowtie wobbled with glee,
Complaining of prickles, oh dear, woe is me!
He ordered a latte from a passing bee,
Who buzzed back with honey, "Now isn't that sweet?"

As the sun set low, a parade of sights,
Ants in a conga line, what a delight!
They marched to a tune only they could hear,
And we all joined in with a joyful cheer!

Magic Lurking in the Underbrush

In the thicket, a frog sings loud,
Dancing with shadows, feeling proud.
A mouse in a bow tie starts to prance,
As fireflies join for a twinkling dance.

Beneath a leaf, a party unfolds,
With acorns as chairs, and tales retold.
The owls in the back laugh till they tear,
While squirrels debate just who has the best hair.

Visions Amidst the Mossy Knoll

A rabbit in spectacles reads a book,
While a hedgehog swipes at a sneaky nook.
They argue about where the cheese may hide,
As laughter echoes, they can't decide.

The breeze brings whispers of tales so wild,
With critters all giggling, nature's own child.
A picnic of thistles, so curious and spry,
With cupcakes made from the fluff in the sky.

Fantasies Framed by Branches

The crows in their coats chatter and squawk,
Holding council beneath a large, stoic rock.
Each feels like a king with a crown of twigs,
As they plot their day full of fun and digs.

A squirrel in slippers flips pancakes blind,
While ants draft the plans that no one can find.
They toast to the sun, and a dance-off begins,
In this leafy arena, everybody wins!

A Tapestry Woven with Stardust

Under the moon, a raccoon plays bass,
While crickets jump in a rhythmic race.
Fireflies blink as if giving a sign,
That tonight is for fun, and all is divine.

Silly shadows of creatures abound,
In this whimsical world, laughter is found.
Each twirl and shimmy, a delight, oh so clear,
As stars laugh along, joining in on the cheer.

The Enchanted Vale Calls

In a vale where the cows wear hats,
And squirrels dance with acrobatic spats,
A rabbit juggles carrots with glee,
While the old owl hoots, 'Come join me!'

The brook laughs at fish that try to fly,
While frogs play chess as time ticks by,
A gnome in a garden falls on his nose,
As daisies giggle and tickle his toes.

Tranquility Under the Leafy Arch

Beneath the trees, there's a parrot's roar,
As chipmunks argue about candy store lore,
Sunbeams tickle the grass with delight,
While ants host a party, all brewing just right.

A lazy bear dreams of honey's sweet charms,
While raccoons practice their latest alarm,
The grasshoppers tap dance, a jazzy invite,
It's a humorous dance in the soft morning light.

Slumbering Colors of the Hidden Grove

In the grove where colors take naps,
Mice wear pajamas, and greet with high claps,
A turtle flips pancakes while birds sing a tune,
While the moon tries to sneak in at noon.

The flowers gossip in whispering tones,
As butterflies discuss their fashion loans,
A dandelion sneezes, a gust of bright gold,
Causing chuckles, as stories unfold.

Threads of Thought in the Twisting Vines

In a tangle of vines, ideas play hide,
As a porcupine tries to find a good slide,
A lizard recites poetry wrapped in a twist,
While the bees wonder how they could miss.

The moon laughs at shadows, playing tag with the sun,
As fish on dry land say, 'This isn't fun!',
A fox with a top hat offers tea by the brook,
And grins while the world gives a perplexed look.

Tides of Thought in the Whispering Woods

In the woods where odd things grow,
Trees converse, but oh so slow.
A squirrel rolls by in a tiny chair,
Chasing shadows without a care.

Mushrooms wear hats, all fancy and bright,
While raccoons plot to steal the moonlight.
Laughter echoes, a whimsical sound,
In this quirky space, joy can be found.

Tales Told by the Twilight Trees

Twilight trees tell tales with glee,
Of a chicken who dreamed to be free.
She danced with frogs on lily pads,
While a cat nearby laughed, feeling glad.

A sleepy owl hooted, "What a sight!"
As unicorns twirled, oh what delight!
They polished their horns till the stars did shine,
In the cool breeze, it felt divine.

Serpentine Paths of Slumbering Hopes

Along the paths where wishes creep,
Worms dip their toes, half-asleep.
A sleepy snail moves with a yawn,
Dreams of racing—oh, by dawn!

A butterfly sneezes, causing a stir,
It stumbles 'round, oh how it did purr!
The fireflies giggle, lighting the way,
While frogs in tuxedos sing, "Hooray!"

A Symphony of Evening Colors

Colors swirl as the sun goes down,
A disco ball spins, could it be a crown?
The flowers droop, taking a bow,
While minnows breakdance in the shallow.

A parrot croons with a touch of sass,
While ants march on in a funky class.
With giggles and grins, the night unfolds,
In this merry land, magic beholds.

Reflections in the Misty Meadow

Bouncing clouds like fluffy sheep,
The daisies giggle, secrets they keep.
A snail pulls a cart with a carrot inside,
While the grasshoppers to the drumbeat abide.

A frog in a tux plays a grand piano,
Notes flutter like butterflies, oh what a show!
The sun winks and shines, tickling the leaves,
As squirrels in bowties plot their grand heaves.

The breeze whispers jokes to the tall, proud trees,
While ants start a dance in perfect freeze.
A rabbit complains, "I'm late for my date!"
With a cat in a hat, and a dance to create!

In this meadow, all things can be,
Including a fox who's the next big MC.
So let's laugh with the flowers, sing with the grass,
And hope that this laughter forever will last.

Enchantment of the Woodland Depths

In the heart of the woods, a dance does arise,
With mushrooms as hats, to everyone's surprise.
A raccoon with flair juggles acorns with glee,
While the owls in the trees hoot, "Just let it be!"

A beetle on stilts walks past all the toadstools,
While butterflies flit by, with the best of their jewels.
The mossy old rocks play cards with the streams,
As fireflies spin tales that glow like our dreams.

The breeze tickles leaves, making soft giggles emerge,
As bushes gossip wildly, they're ready to purge.
With twinkles and sparkles, the woodland takes flight,
Hosting a ball that lasts deep into the night.

Oh, what a sight in this land bizarre,
Where every small creature's a bright shining star!
So grab all your friends and twirl in delight,
For in this wild world, everything feels right.

Reverie Above Rooted Realms

Up in the branches, where the whimsy flies,
A parrot tells stories with clever disguise.
A turtle in shades chills out on a limb,
While the chipmunks create a pop band so dim.

Roving raccoons are the kings of this scene,
Flaunting their treasures—a candy machine!
With gumdrops for wheels and a lollipop steering,
They zoom through the trees, and you can hear cheering!

Among the tall trunks, a stand-up parade,
With beetles in bow ties serenading the shade.
The sun tickles branches, making shadows dance,
While weaving through laughter, we're caught in a trance.

In this rooted realm, all worries set free,
Laughter's the festival, come join the spree!
Where even the roots wear party hats tight,
Celebrating all day and glowing with light.

Fantasies in the Fern-filled Folds

Down in the ferns, where the mischief is thick,
A hedgehog spins tales, he's quite the slick.
A caterpillar leans back, living fast,
While the dragonflies gossip, rumors are cast.

A party unfolds with cakes made of moss,
Filled with sweet nectar, everyone's the boss.
The bumblebees dance to the hum of the beat,
As ants provide rhythm with tiny little feet.

In this hidden fold, the laughter's so loud,
Even shy fawns gather, joining the crowd.
With fireflies twinkling like stars in a race,
They twirl through the night with intricate grace.

So come take a stroll through the ferns by the brook,
Where the craziest tales can easily cook.
In this whimsical world, let your heart play its role,
As laughter and joy fill your very soul.

The Gentle Pull of Twilight

As dusk draws nigh, the frogs do croak,
Their ribbits sound like a silly joke.
The fireflies twirl in a jittery waltz,
While crickets chirp like they're here by default.

The moon peeks out from behind a cloud,
It seems to giggle, all cheeky and proud.
Stars wink at us, a cheeky parade,
In this twilight carnival, none feel afraid.

The owls hoot softly, but wear a grin,
While shadows play tag, letting chaos begin.
A rabbit hops by, wearing a top hat,
In this funny hour, we're all part of that.

So raise a glass to the silly night,
Where laughter mingles with fading light.
In the valley of whims, we'll frolic and play,
For in this sweet twilight, we'll lose our way.

Mirth Among the Marshes

In the marsh where the quacking ducks parade,
They swim in circles like a funny charade.
With their flappy feet, they dance in a line,
Creating a splash while looking divine.

The cattails whisper their secrets with glee,
While turtles practice their best comedy.
If frogs wore glasses, they'd read the news,
About the latest gaffes of their silly crew.

A beaver, a jester, builds dams with flair,
Shooting water high with a joyous air.
In our marshy realm, laughter's a must,
As nature's antics build whimsical trust.

So let's gather here, in the marsh's embrace,
Laughing at life in this frolicking space.
For every odd critter adds to the fun,
Creating a scene that's second to none.

Secrets in the Swaying Grass

Amidst the blades that bob and sway,
The grasshoppers jump with a hop and play.
They debate which leaf makes a proper bed,
While passing the time on their green, leafy thread.

Bees buzz in chorus, a cacophony bright,
Their tiny dance puts the sun to flight.
While a snail takes a selfie, slow but sincere,
In the realm of the grass, there's much to revere.

A shy field mouse tosses a crumb to a friend,
They chuckle together, their giggles ascend.
In this grassy palace of secrets and cheer,
Life's little wonders are all gathered here.

So come, sit with me, where the wild things bloom,
Together we'll weave joy and tackle the gloom.
For every hidden laugh in the swaying grass,
Is a treasure uncovered as moments pass.

Flights of Fancy

Up in the air, where the kites take wing,
The children all cheer as their laughter does sing.
With strings all tangled, they tumble and swirl,
In a whirlwind of colors, their spirits unfurl.

A squirrel on a branch tries to join in the fun,
Chasing the kites till the daylight is done.
While sparrows remark on the sights from above,
The whole world below is a treasure trove of love.

Paper birds soar, with a flap and a twist,
Each one a dream, too good to resist.
While a playful breeze tickles our cheeks,
In this whimsical flight, it's laughter that speaks.

So let's soar together, on this journey bright,
With giggles and dreams, from morning till night.
For every flight leads to laughter and play,
In the skies of our hearts, where we dance and sway.

Glimpses of Enchantment Behind the Bark

In a world where squirrels wear hats,
And rabbits dance like acrobats.
Bees buzz tunes from tiny bands,
While mushrooms play in enchanted lands.

A mouse in boots plays a tiny lute,
While snails glide by in a grand pursuit.
The trees gossip in whispers and shrieks,
As sunlight confuses the shy little peaks.

Lizards tell tales of the days gone by,
As fireflies twinkle a flickering sigh.
Here, the unexpected is always near,
In this quirky place where laughter's sincere.

A Haven Where Imaginations Roam

A frog in a tie sings opera so loud,
As butterflies gather, forming a crowd.
Clouds wear faces and make funny jokes,
As wise old owls recite silly folks.

The moon throws a party in the tree tops,
With stars in blazers and twinkling props.
The forest is lively with giggles and cheer,
As imagination spins tales, profound yet clear.

A gnome on a swing flies higher than dreams,
While raccoons chew popcorn and plot their schemes.
In this magical place, where thoughts come alive,
Laughter reigns, and the silly things thrive.

Adventures in the Dappled Light

In patches of sunlight, mischief galore,
Cats dressed as ninjas are hard to ignore.
The groundhogs practice their ballet skills,
While chipmunks debate on the best of meals.

The grass tickles toes as the laughter erupts,
While fireflies dance, and the world disrupts.
A woodpecker pulls pranks on the shy little deer,
And a snail dreams of zooming with speed without fear.

Amidst dappled light, and shadows so bold,
Stories of wonders and laughs unfold.
Here, in the wilderness where giggles collide,
Adventures abound with joy as our guide.

Shadows Cradled in the Forest Floor

Beneath the tall trees, shadows play tricks,
As the groundhog gives hiccuping kicks.
A squirrel, all jolly, hoards nuts in a tree,
Whispers to shadows, 'Come swing here with me!'

The sun winks at flowers, all dressed in their best,
While ants in a line take a leisurely quest.
In the quiet, a beetle joins in with a tune,
Creating a ruckus beneath the blue moon.

The leaves laugh softly, as stories unwind,
Of escapades dreamy and one of a kind.
With humor embraced in the soft forest glow,
Life dances gently, in the ebb and flow.

Serenade of the Forest Shade

In wild woods where squirrels chat,
A bear wears shades and a fancy hat.
The rabbits waltz in a leafy ball,
Chasing butterflies, having a ball.

A pig plays tunes on a twig-made flute,
While foxes groove in their Sunday suit.
The owls hoot in a comical way,
As branches sway in a leafy ballet.

Frogs croak out jokes in the evening glow,
While fireflies flash, putting on a show.
The raccoons clap to the beat with flair,
As the night buzzes with whimsical air.

And when dawn breaks, they all disappear,
Leaving the laughter for the dawn to hear.
In the hush of the morn, nature will smile,
For magic awaits in a thousand ways, all the while.

Secrets Beneath the Canopy

Under the leaves, where silliness reigns,
A tortoise once danced in the muddy lanes.
The hedgehogs shared secrets with the trees,
While ants formed conga lines, if you please!

A chipmunk juggled acorns with glee,
While a raccoon painted, 'Look at me!'
The parakeets giggled, sharing the news,
Of squirrels making fuzzy, colorful shoes.

Down in the roots, wise owls plot schemes,
Setting up shows under moonlight beams.
With starlight glinting on dew-kissed grass,
They throw the wildest parties for all to pass.

A hedgehog chef cooks pies with a twist,
As frogs guide the dance, you can't resist.
For beneath the canopy, laughter runs free,
In nature's own circus, come join the spree!

Lullabies of the Emerald Hollow

In the hollow, the crickets sing soft,
While dancing shadows tease the aloft.
A sleepy bear snores, using a log,
As frogs strum banjos, proclaiming, "No fog!"

The wise old tree tells tales with a grin,
Of naughty squirrels and their wild spin.
A nightingale hums in a leafy plight,
As stars wink down, adding to the night.

Toadstools gather, hosting a tea,
Inviting all creatures, come share a spree.
The fireflies twinkle like tiny stars,
As all join in for fun, including guitars.

And as the moon weaves silver in skies,
Laughter echoes, under yawns and sighs.
In emerald hollow, joy goes on mute,
But whispers of fun forever take root.

Murmurs of the Starlit Glade

In the glade, the shadows play tricks,
As shadows weave with the moonlit flicks.
A bumbling bear trips on his own paws,
While laughter erupts, sharing simple flaws.

A sleek weasel twirls with flair and grace,
While badgers join in, keeping up the pace.
The hedgehog croons sweet songs so bold,
As the night wraps snugly in stories retold.

With giggles echoing, the owls critique,
'Not a smooth flier,' they jointly speak.
Beneath the stars, they giggle and tease,
For in such moments, worries just freeze.

A porcupine juggles acorns galore,
While rabbits hop in through the backdoor.
As dawn hints softly, they'll fade out of sight,
But in starlit glades, fun lingers bright!

Starlight on the Hollow

In the hollow where shadows sway,
Silly critters dance and play,
A raccoon in a top hat struts,
While squirrels cheer with little nuts.

Moonbeams twinkle, the night's a show,
With a frog on a lily, stealing the glow,
They twirl and leap, with joyful zest,
Who knew the woods could be such a jest?

Crickets chirp with a rhythmic jab,
As a hedgehog spins, hitting a cab,
Each twirl and giggle echo the air,
In this strange land, there's fun to spare.

With a wink from the owl in the bright,
Who joins in on this silly night,
As starlight hits the hollow ground,
Laughter echoes all around.

Breezes of a Forgotten Haven

In a haven where breezes tease,
Rusty signs dance with glee and ease,
A mouse in shoes, they think it's chic,
Wobbly steps make the ground squeak.

Trees whisper secrets to the breeze,
While a lazy cat snoozes with ease,
A parrot drops puns from a height,
Making everyone giggle in pure delight.

A lost flip-flop sings a tune,
The flowers sway, they're in the mood,
Butterflies gather for a grand feast,
Sipping nectar, they come in twos.

With each gust, mischief does spread,
A tumbleweed rolls, it's well-fed,
In this forgotten spot, oh so fine,
Life is a joke — and laughter's divine.

Visions of a Hidden Glen

In the glen where mischief brews,
Giggling snails wear tiny shoes,
A turtle on a skateboard zooms,
While rabbits plot their silly plumes.

With daisies dressed in hats so grand,
They orchestrate a waltz on land,
A hedgehog serenades the trees,
As flowers nod in cheerful tease.

A frog with dreams of Broadway fame,
Practices a dance, forgetting his name,
The crickets applaud with tiny limbs,
While the brook just chuckles and softly swims.

As night wraps the glen in its cloak,
The stars peek out for a little joke,
Their twinkle sends ripples of cheer,
In this hidden glen, it's all about fun here.

The Lullaby of the Landscape

In the landscape where giggles meet,
A cow in pajamas lumbers with fleet,
The chicken croons with a feathered flair,
While the sun just chuckles, basking in air.

Tall wheat dances in a playful line,
As clouds drift by, composing a rhyme,
A duck leads a parade on the lane,
Quacking tunes that tickle the brain.

As night falls calm, the fireflies glow,
They play tag with wishes that float to and fro,
Beneath starlit skies, the laughter rolls,
In this landscape, joy embraces our souls.

With lullabies sung by rustling grass,
The critters laugh as the moments pass,
Each corner whispers a comical tale,
In the heart of the land, fun will prevail.

The Enchanted Vale

In the vale where cows wear hats,
Silly goats engage in chats.
Beneath the trees, the rabbits dance,
While hedgehogs join in the prance.

A frog in specs reads a book,
And claims he's quite the clever cook.
Frolicking, the squirrels toss nuts,
While birds chirp out their funny cuts.

A snail with dreams of running fast,
Takes a break and hopes to last.
He plans a trip to see the sun,
But finds it hard to have some fun.

The stream giggles as it flows,
Tickling toes while everyone knows.
In this vale, the joy runs free,
Oh what a place for you and me!

Echoes of the Quiet Grove

In the grove where whispers play,
The trees tell tales in a funny way.
A raccoon juggles acorns high,
While squirrels plot to make him cry.

The owl wears glasses, quite absurd,
And reads aloud the silliest word.
A chipmunk tries a magic trick,
But ends up with a sticky stick.

Underneath the moon's sly grin,
The fireflies join a gleeful din.
They dance around a patch of grass,
Enticing everyone to pass.

With laughter echoing through the night,
The grove becomes a silly sight.
If you should wander, come and hear,
The giggles of the friends so dear.

Fantasies Among the Pines

By the pines, a cat in shades,
Sips tea while munching on some blades.
He thinks he's cool, all laid-back fine,
But loses his cup, it's quite the sign.

The beavers build a castle grand,
While otters slide just like they planned.
A turtle dreams of winning races,
While frogs poke fun at all his paces.

The squirrels throw a wacky bash,
With jellybeans and lots of trash.
They dance like no one's watching near,
In the pines, there's nothing to fear.

The moon shines down, a silver light,
As critters laugh through the cold night.
Among the pines, a joy divine,
Where every tree has its own sign.

Shadows of a Hushed Night

In the night, the shadows creep,
Where crickets whisper, secrets keep.
A bear in pajamas, fast asleep,
Dreams of honey and endless sheep.

A raccoon wearing a tiny crown,
Trots around, but then falls down.
The fireflies giggle, blink, and sway,
As they light up the bear's ballet.

The hedgehogs waltz in tiny shoes,
Ignoring all the nighttime blues.
With laughter echoing, dreams take flight,
Underneath the soft, starry light.

In the hush, a parade begins,
With critters bursting out in grins.
When shadows fade, the fun won't wane,
For in this night, joy's never plain.

Whispers of the Meadow

In the grass, a tickle hides,
As the rabbits do their slides.
Flowers giggle, petals dance,
Underneath the sun's bright glance.

Butterflies wear silly hats,
Chasing shadows, teasing rats.
Bees hum tunes, a buzzing band,
Playing jigs across the land.

Worms in bow ties wiggle low,
Singing songs that none can know.
The daisies clap and cheer them on,
While the mice strut till the dawn.

Silly squirrels make a fuss,
Riding on a train of bus.
Nature's laughter fills the air,
In this meadow, joy to share.

Secrets Beneath the Stars

Beneath the sky, a fox is sly,
With a twinkle in his eye.
He tells tales of nighttime quirks,
As his tail in circles lurks.

Owls wear glasses, wise and round,
Spread their data, all profound.
Crickets chirp a tune of fun,
While fireflies play tag and run.

Stars might wink, but don't you peep,
As the raccoons laugh, and leap.
They'll steal your snacks, a thrilling show,
With giggles floating soft and low.

Mice in tuxes hold a ball,
Cheese platters set, they part and call.
The night unfolds, full and bright,
With secrets shared and pure delight.

Moonlit Reveries

In the glow, the shadows prance,
Trees are swaying, birds in trance.
A raccoon dons a silver crown,
As the sleepy sun goes down.

Bunnies bounce in moonlight's gleam,
Chasing stardust in a dream.
Hares play hopscotch on the grass,
With giggles that the night won't pass.

The owls hoot with a clever jest,
"Who will join our nightly quest?"
With froggy leaps and merry cheers,
They dance away all creeping fears.

Stars above in winding trails,
Listen close to fuzzy tales.
In this night, with moonlight's cheer,
All is fun, no room for fear.

Reflections in the Glade

In a glade where laughter flows,
Squirrels juggling acorns pose.
Fairies giggle, sparkles fly,
Telling tales to the sky.

Pansies sport the latest trends,
While the thyme plays tricks with friends.
A chipmunk wears a fancy coat,
Hopping off to share a note.

Willy-nilly, wild and free,
Turtles dance on leaves of tea.
Hummingbirds in top hats zoom,
Swirling dreams around the bloom.

All these wonders, nighttime's laugh,
Nature draws a happy graph.
In the glade, with joy we wade,
Life's a game, by laughter made.

Celestial Whimsy

In the meadow, cows wear crowns,
Chasing butterflies in silly gowns.
A rabbit hops with shoes so bright,
Holding court till the fall of night.

Squirrels debate on acorn stocks,
While frogs perform in dapper frocks.
The sun winks down, a goofy grin,
As the flowers dance, their petals spin.

A wise old owl starts a jest,
Telling tales of the feathered quest.
The moon giggles, twinkling high,
As stars applaud with a twinkly sigh.

Tides of the Imagined Land

Out on the beach, a crab wears shades,
Surfing waves like it won the grades.
Seagulls squawk a comical tune,
While shells compete for the sun's best boon.

Fish throw a party, bubbles fly,
As dolphins leap, oh my, oh my!
Jellyfish glow like disco lights,
Inviting all to dance through nights.

A clam tells jokes, with a nervous grin,
While the ocean laughs, its laughter spins.
The sand tickles toes in a playful joke,
As seaweed sways, the party's stoked!

The Lure of Untold Stories

A coyote sits with a pencil and pad,
Writing tales that make him glad.
The deer roll eyes, scoff at the lines,
While critters giggle, sharing their signs.

In a hollow log, a raccoon reads,
Comics about adventurous deeds.
The stars conspire, hear tales of yore,
As fireflies sketch on the forest floor.

A turtle spins yarns, slow but grand,
While cheeky chipmunks lend a hand.
The night is young, full of delight,
As whispers weave through the silver light.

A Chorus of Petals

In a garden where flowers sing,
Roses and daisies do their thing.
A sunflower shakes to a funky beat,
While violets sway on their little feet.

Butterflies flit in a whimsical dance,
As bees buzz in a polka romance.
Laughter ripples through verdant stems,
With tulips playing hide and hems.

Dandelions blow puffs of cheer,
Each seed a wish on the breeze near.
Petunias giggle, making a fuss,
As the whole garden joins in the trust.

Shadows of the Meadow's Embrace

In a field where shadows play,
A cat wears shades on a sunny day.
Butterflies dance with silly grace,
While rabbits hop in a merry race.

A squirrel juggles acorns around,
As silly laughter echoes the ground.
The flowers giggle in a breeze,
Tickled by the whispers of trees.

Tall grass tickles the toes you see,
As frogs sing out their symphony.
The sun beams down, a bright scarf's hue,
The meadow's antics pull you askew.

Chasing rainbows just for fun,
With every minute, joy's begun.
This grassy stage of merriment spills,
With shadows laughing in quirky thrills.

Melodies of the Mystic Dell

In a dell where the oddballs gather,
A fox recites jokes that make you lather.
The trees sway left with a goofy grin,
As birds chirp tunes that make heads spin.

A big bumbling bear tries to dance,
Tripping over vines in a funny prance.
The brook chuckles as it flows by,
As silly scenes unfold, oh my!

A raccoon reads a book upside down,
While a turtle wears a tiny crown.
The laughter echoes through the moss,
In this enchanted place, we're at a gloss.

Each melody brings a chuckle or two,
They tickle the heart in skies so blue.
Mystical fun waits for every guest,
In this whirlwind of joy, we're truly blessed.

Imagining Beneath the Cedar Bough

Beneath a bough where the giggles reside,
A lizard in a vest puts on a slide.
Chickens wear hats made of feathers and fluff,
Telling tall tales that are just quite tough.

A bear with a bowtie spins stories bold,
Of treasure maps and wizards of old.
He trips on a vine, then rolls with glee,
As laughter erupts with each shimmy spree.

The wind chimes in with a melody sweet,
While rabbits tap dance on their little feet.
Beneath the cedar, the silliness flows,
With every rustle, the fun just grows.

Imagining worlds where whimsy's abound,
With whimsy and wackiness all around.
The forest joins in, with a clap and cheer,
For the joy of the moment is perfectly clear.

Illusions in the Thicket's Whisper

In the twilight, secrets unfurl,
As owls wear spectacles in a twirl.
The thicket giggles with whispers bright,
While chipmunks play hide-and-seek at night.

A grumpy goat strums an old guitar,
As fireflies twinkle like a movie star.
The trees sway gently, a funny sight,
With shadows dancing in the soft moonlight.

A raccoon's got an act to show,
That makes you roll, oh what a flow!
Illusions sprout in this quirky nook,
With laughter echoing like a storybook.

The thicket sings of joy so profound,
As night creatures join in with a merry sound.
In a world of wonders and playful cheer,
The heart feels light as laughter draws near.

Woodland Wonders of the Wistful Night

The squirrels wear hats made of leaves,
And dance on the branches with such ease.
A rabbit juggles acorns with flair,
While owls hoot jokes that float in the air.

Fireflies flicker like stars that confide,
Whispering secrets as critters collide.
A raccoon sings opera, clad in a shawl,
With a frog as his perch, oh, what a ball!

The moon rolls her eyes at the scene below,
As chipmunks perform in a brave little show.
Each bush has a giggle, each tree holds a grin,
In this silly spectacle, let laughter begin!

With shadows that waltz and the breeze that plays,
Every critter joins in the merriest phase.
In forests alive with mischief and cheer,
The woodland's a stage, let's all gather near!

Fragments of Light in the Rustic Grotto

In a cave where bat families dwell,
A munchy bat hoards a candy-filled shell.
He offers a caramel, sticky and sweet,
While a hedgehog rolls by on its tiny little feet.

There's laughter that bounces off wall and dome,
As a badger brings tea and a quirky old tome.
The mice play charades with their minuscule flair,
A dance-off erupts as they puff out their hair.

Crickets compose tunes with a twist of their wings,
While frogs dive for gigs where the music just sings.
The glowworms shine like tiny disco balls,
As laughter erupts from the roots in the halls.

So join in the frolic, the joy and the fun,
In this grotto of wonders, the night's just begun!
With fragments of light, it's a sight to behold,
In the heart of the darkness, true magic unfolds.

Echoing Lullabies of the Shaded Dell

In a dell where the whispers of laughter combine,
A turtle crochets a bright quilt of sunshine.
He knits all the colors from grass, sky, and flower,
While a snail conducts tunes with meticulous power.

There's giggles and grins from a fox on a swing,
As he shouts out tall tales of wild, wacky things.
The owls take their seats for the puppet play show,
With shadows shifting slyly, their expressions aglow.

A raccoon's the director, he wears a grand hat,
With acorns as props and a seat for a bat.
The audience chuckles at each silly line,
In this charming, bright dell, everything's fine!

As stars twinkle down in a quiet embrace,
All creatures unite in this snug, happy space.
So come, take a seat, and let laughter swell,
In the chorus of joy that the night's going to tell!

Fables Spun Beneath the Wildwood Sky

Underneath the wide, wobbly sky,
A parrot tells tales that seem to fly by.
With acorn crowns styled in the silliest way,
Each fable a giggle, a twist, and a play.

A fox writes a story with ink made of dew,
While a squirrel's on stage giving acorns their due.
The trees sway along, with their branches like friends,
In this quirky theater where laughter transcends.

The crickets sing harmony, starry-eyed nights,
While fireflies flash in matching light tights.
Each creature takes turns, with pride in their hearts,
Bringing forth laughter in whimsical parts.

So lean in and listen, with joy on your face,
To fables of laughter in this magical place.
Under wildwood's gaze, let your worries all fly,
Join the fun-telling creatures beneath the sly sky!

Paintings of the Mind in Nature's Embrace

In fields so bright, a cow wears shades,
While squirrels dance in fancy parades.
A butterfly winks, paints clouds so queer,
And whispers to flowers, "Let's drink a beer!"

The trees paint stripes with a goofy grin,
And rabbits hop by with a ukulele spin.
The sun does a jig, the clouds just laugh,
As nature plays host to a jolly staff.

Bouncing blooms throw a confetti show,
While bees join in with a hip-hop flow.
A wind band plays on its wild saxophone,
While birds fly by in zany cartoon tone.

With swaying grass and farcical skies,
Each leaf holds a joke, a comical surprise.
In this whimsical world, all laughter aligns,
Where every corner holds playful designs.

Whispers of the Past in the Glistening Leaves

Old trees gossip like grannies at noon,
While acorns are giggling, who knew?
Dancing shadows recount their tales,
As chipmunks shop in their tiny veils.

The brook cracks jokes on the pebbles' heads,
While frogs wear bow ties, it's all in their threads.
A wind chime clinks in slapstick laughter,
Saying, "Catch the breeze— it's always after!"

All the squirrels plot their next big stunt,
As a snail drags its house, on the run, to hunt.
Leaves rustle cheekily, sharing their pranks,
While a hedgehog gives high fives with its ranks.

In the glistening air where the past leans old,
Every giggle told is worth its weight in gold.
With whispers of joy that time cannot quell,
Nature awaits with stories to tell.

The Secret Life of Sylvan Shadows

Under the moon, shadows throw a ball,
With owls as referees, it's a hoot for all.
Frogs wear tuxedos, all prim and spry,
While fireflies flicker like stars in the sky.

The shadows twist and turn in delight,
As crickets sing stanzas all through the night.
Mice wear their tiny party hats,
As shadows play chess with the chubby rats.

In corners where sunlight dares not to tread,
The forest holds secrets of laughter instead.
From thickets to glades, with a twinkle and sigh,
The shadows unite under a giggling sky.

When dawn begins peeking, the shadows all fade,
But whispers remain of the games that they played.
As light fills the woods with its golden throne,
The echoes of laughter stay— never alone.

Flickering Lights in the Twilight Hideaway

In the garden, lanterns twinkle with cheer,
Frogs leap like dancers, spreading good vibes here.
Bats in top hats pull off a sly show,
As fireflies wiggle in a soft glow.

Hares toast with carrots, raising them high,
While owls laugh heartily, asking, "Why not try?"
A raccoon juggles berries in a spree,
While hedgehogs cheer, "Bigger spills for me!"

Crickets play violins made of twigs,
In this twilight hideaway, full of jigs.
Each flicker of light, a wink in disguise,
As shadows join in, blushing with surprise.

In the breeze, the evening sings like a bard,
With giggles and murmurs, never too hard.
The night wraps its arms, so cozy and bright,
In the flickering glow of twilight's delight.

The Sylvan State of Wishful Thinking

In the woods where squirrels plot,
And the birds play silly tricks,
A tree once lost its dancing shoes,
Now it's swaying in the mix.

The rabbits hold a laughing spree,
Chasing shadows on the ground,
While the flowers gossip softly,
In petals where the joy is found.

A bear's got hiccups, he does twirl,
Spilling honey on the ants,
They're taken aback, a sticky mess,
Headed for a ballet dance.

Mice in top hats join the fun,
With tiny canes, they prance about,
A festival of giggles glows,
In a realm where laughter shouts.

Blossoming Wishes Under the Canopy

Beneath the boughs, a toad sings high,
While fireflies jump, all aglow,
The daisies wave their arms so wide,
Inviting all to put on a show.

A chipmunk juggles acorns with flair,
As squirrels cheer and clap their paws,
The breeze is filled with joyous notes,
As nature gives its full applause.

A wise old owl hoots a riddle
To the throng of woodland cheers,
They crack up at its silly speech,
Earnest answers drown in jeers.

Each flower holds a joke inside,
Telling tales of their sprightly bloom,
For every petal's got a punchline,
Transforming the frown to room.

Whimsies in the Twilight Breeze

When twilight wraps the trees in gold,
The shadows stretch and softly giggle,
An echo of the whispered tales,
That make the nighttime critters wiggle.

A hedgehog wears a tiny hat,
With feathers that sway and dance,
He tips it low to passersby,
Inviting all for a chance romanced.

A fox plays chess with a wise old bat,
Each move is riddled with spiteful glee,
While crickets serenade the crowd,
Playing tunes of light-hearted spree.

Stars begin to clap in delight,
As the moon shines like a grand cake,
In this lore-filled, funny milieu,
The night gives all more laughs to take.

The Melodic Pulse of Nature's Heart

In nature's realm, a tune is spun,
With chirps that tickle ears in flight,
The rivers laugh, a bubbling song,
As frogs debate the stars at night.

The wind carries a playful jest,
As branches sway with silly grace,
And daisies join in with a laugh,
Each little bud a smiling face.

A porcupine pirouettes slow,
While ladybugs form a conga line,
As snails slide in with gentle flair,
Under the moon's comedic shine.

The chorus grows, a party's here,
Each critter adds its quirky part,
In this joyful, vibrant symphony,
Resounds the pulse of nature's heart.

The Stillness of Lost Paths

In a field where grass does sway,
A chicken crossed, but lost its way.
It clucked in circles, quite confused,
While butterflies just laughed and booed.

Beneath the trees, a hedgehog rolled,
Thinking it was bold and bold.
But every time it tried to dash,
It ended up in quite the crash!

The flowers whispered jokes so bright,
While crickets played their songs at night.
When frogs in suits began to dance,
The fireflies lit up in a prance.

Oh, the paths here twist and twirl,
With mischief hiding in each swirl.
So join the fun, don't fade away,
In this silliness, let's laugh and play!

The Unseen Wonders of the Night.

The stars above were quite a sight,
As jellybeans flew left and right.
A moonlit ball of quirky fun,
With owls that dared to dance and run.

A raccoon wearing boots so bold,
Sang songs about sweet pies of gold.
While badgers jogged in silly hats,
And shared their snacks with jumping rats.

The shadows stretched and pulled a prank,
As lanterns bobbed and sidekicks drank.
With giggles lost in the cool breeze,
The night became a joyful tease.

Through beams of light that flicker bright,
They chased their dreams till morning light.
In every nook, a giggle grew,
For nighttime secrets much too few.

Whispers of the Moonlit Grove

In a grove where whispers play,
A squirrel tripped and fell all day.
With acorns rolling, laughter rang,
As cattle grazed while the crickets sang.

A crooked tree with branches wide,
Held a raccoon, quite full of pride.
He wore a crown made out of twigs,
And challenged all the frogs to jigs!

Fireflies flickered, joined the cheer,
Creating lights that brought no fear.
For in this grove of playful tunes,
Even the owls danced under moons.

So come, let's twirl in nature's glow,
With every critter joining the show!
In moonlit dreams, we'll jump and twine,
In the whimsy of this goofy pine.

Echoes in the Twilight Thicket

In twilight thickets, shadows creep,
While giggling goats make quite the leap.
With hats too big and tails that sway,
They twirled around in their own play.

A bear with glasses read a book,
While mice planned pranks from their nook.
When fireflies held a glow parade,
The night turned bright as laughter played.

A hedgehog made a superhero cap,
And every creature planned a map.
In echoes of the rustling trees,
Came tales of joy carried by the breeze.

So come and join this funny frolic,
In the thicket's wild, a silly topic!
With laughter shared till dusk turns deep,
In this merry world where we can leap!

Within the Cool Embrace

In a shady nook, where squirrels prance,
A game of tag, a silly dance.
Butterflies flutter, with twinkling flair,
While frogs croak jokes, without a care.

The tall grass giggles, sways with glee,
As rabbits plot their mystery spree.
A gopher peeks from his muddy hole,
Winks at the sun, feeling quite whole.

Picnic ants march, hats on their heads,
Stealing crumbs from sleepy threads.
The breeze whispers, a tickling tease,
As daisies sway, doing the twist with ease.

Underneath the trees, it's quite a sight,
A parade of giggles, from morn till night.
Laughter echoes, nature's song,
In the cool embrace, where all belong.

Nightfall's Gentle Caress

As twilight wraps the world in fun,
Fireflies waltz, a glowing run.
Owls wear glasses, looking so wise,
While raccoons plot under starry skies.

Cool shadows play, teasing the light,
Chasing the crickets, a silly flight.
The moon chuckles, a skewed grin bright,
As a cat stumbles, in the soft night.

Mice in pajamas, having a ball,
Join in the dance, just tiny and small.
Every branch is a stage, every leaf a fan,
In the nightfall's glow, a whimsical plan.

Under the canopy, giggles grow loud,
A gathering of joy that's ever so proud.
In the dark's embrace, it's all just a jest,
Where laughter echoes, and all are blessed.

Fables in Ferns

By the ferns' fronds, tales take flight,
Where beetles tell stories, with all their might.
A lizard in slippers, a sight to behold,
Recites ancient legends, both funny and bold.

The butterflies gossip, in bright shades of glee,
Sharing secrets of who kissed the bee.
While the spiders spin yarns, so intricate and fine,
About the great dance of the old green vine.

A caterpillar's dream of a bold comeback,
Turns into laughter, then a snack attack.
Each fern sways gently, in whimsical tone,
Creating a world where silliness is grown.

Nestled in moss, under twinkling light,
Fables emerge, spilling joy and delight.
A gathering of critters, both big and small,
In this ferny realm, there's room for all.

A Tapestry of Light and Leaf

Every leaf a canvas, under sun's bright laugh,
Where shadows and sunshine draw a silly path.
Frogs in tuxedos croak a funky song,
While the daisies sway, joining along.

There's a breeze that tickles, a playful sneer,
As birds mimic laughter, filling the sphere.
A squirrel with acorns, plotting a feast,
While turtles take bets, to see who's the least.

Beneath the branches, a jester is found,
With wildberries strung, all around.
A giggling brook joins in the festivities,
Carving through stones with whimsical ease.

As day turns to night, the giggles remain,
In a tapestry woven, where fun is the gain.
Every color shines bright, in this leafy domain,
An endless adventure, free of disdain.

The Stillness of Outlandish Whispers

In a place where the goats wear hats,
And rabbits perform silly dance mats,
The trees wear socks, in a stylish way,
As the cows plot music, night and day.

Llamas recite poems in high squeaky tones,
While squirrels play chess with their shiny old bones,
A turtle spins tales of a grand, wild chase,
With a pie on his head, he owns the whole place.

A fox in a tuxedo stirs up some tea,
While owls spin around like they're lost by a spree,
The air is thick with laughter and cheer,
In this wild haven, there's nothing to fear.

So join the parade of the giggling beasts,
In a world full of odd, comical feasts,
Where whispers abound in colors so bright,
A jest in the stillness, a curious sight.

Chromatic Fantasies in Nature's Caress

Butterflies don shades, a whimsical crowd,
While flowers wear sneakers, all lively and loud,
The sun paints the sky with a smile so wide,
As puddles reflect all the joy inside.

The grass grows tall and sprinkles confetti,
Where hedgehogs ride bikes, looking all petty,
The breeze carries giggles from fairies at play,
As clouds peek around, just to join in the fray.

In shadows of trees, bright colors conspire,
To tickle the senses, to tease and inspire,
With each rustle of leaves, laughter fills the air,
While ants throw a party without any care.

So dance with the blooms, in this radiant spree,
Forget the dull world, and just wander free,
For in every corner, absurdity's found,
In this playful realm, joy knows no bound.

Breaths of Serenity in Clusters of Green

Where mossy rocks grumble, and crickets compose,
The bushes throw shade as the sun barely glows,
There's calm in the chaos, a curious sight,
Where giggles emerge with the fall of the night.

A raccoon with glasses, so wise and so spry,
Makes puns with the owls, who hoot: "Oh me, my!"
The whispers of breezes send chuckles around,
In the heart of the glades, joy's easily found.

The ferns hold a chat with the passing old streams,
While snails race their shells in the land of dreams,
Each critter partakes in this silly ballet,
As the stars wink with glee, 'come join the foray!'

In clusters of green, life's a playful jest,
With laughter and peace, we are truly blessed,
So linger a while, let your worries take flight,
In this merry domain, everything feels right.

Parables Written on the Surface of Leaves

On parchment of green, stories etched, just for fun,
A frog in a vest leaps, 'Hey, look! I can run!'
While beetles recount tales in quirky old prose,
With puns and high-fives, they strike silly poses.

The wind carries secrets, untold and absurd,
As chipmunks weave dreams, their laughter's preferred,
Each leaf tells a joke in a rustling cheer,
As flowers respond with a wink and a leer.

There's wisdom in giggles from creatures so small,
Who gather around for a sunny free-for-all,
Each blade of grass whispers a quirk in its sway,
In this wild narrative, let's dance and play.

So tiptoe through stories, on the surface so bright,
Where life's little follies fill hearts with delight,
For in this grand tale, with each twist and turn,
The joy of connection will always return.

Pictures of Reality in a Dreamy Grove

In the grove where squirrels dance,
They wear tiny hats and prance.
Rabbits hop in two-step time,
While leaves giggle, a silly rhyme.

Under trees of candy strips,
Birds are hosting tea party trips.
With cupcakes, pies, and lemonade,
A charmed world of fun brigade.

Yet the owl tries to be the chef,
Burning toast, what a silly mess!
The hedgehogs roll their eyes in glee,
As ants march by with tea for three.

In this grove of playful cheer,
Reality takes a funny steer.
When dreams come alive in bouts of jest,
It's a world where laughter is the best.

Unveiling the Secrets of the Verdant Veil

Peeking through the leafy screen,
A gnome is juggling beans like a machine.
Frogs are croaking fashion tips,
While moonlight laughs at their quirk flips.

The flowers gossip, swaying wide,
About the bugs that love to hide.
In this land where oddities grow,
Silly antics steal the show.

The wise old fox crochets at night,
Knitting scarves from pure moonlight.
While turtles race with shells in tow,
Chasing dreams without a show.

In this vibrant, verdant scene,
The weirdness reigns as the unseen.
With laughter echoing through the leaves,
It's a place where fun never leaves.

The Realm Where Wishes Take Flight

In a field where wishes soar,
The butterflies shout, 'Let's explore!'
With candy clouds and jellybean rain,
The laughter here is never plain.

Penguins play in a pool of goo,
Skating around in a comical crew.
While dandelions burst into cheer,
With a burst of confetti from far and near.

The dreams parade in a silly line,
With talking pies that sip on wine.
Chasing after their starlit fleet,
It's a wild, whimsical, funny treat.

As wishes spread on paper wings,
The whole realm melodiously sings.
In this land where joy is bright,
Every wish takes a laugh-filled flight.

Traces of Abandon in the Woodland Dreamscape

In the woods where shadows play,
Finding traces of yesterday.
Forgotten toys and musical chairs,
Chirping crickets, silly affairs.

A rocking horse starts to sway,
While frogs croon a hit parade.
The trees creak tales of jest and cheer,
In this landscape, fun draws near.

Marshmallows growing on the vines,
With chocolate rivers and candy pines.
Laughter echoes where dreams take hold,
As the woodland whispers laughter bold.

Though abandoned, it's not forlorn,
With sprites frolicking since the morn.
In this dreamscape of goofy grace,
Every trace smiles, hugs, and plays.

www.ingramcontent.com/pod-product-compliance
Lightning Source LLC
Chambersburg PA
CBHW072138200426
43209CB00050B/121